A Christmas Blessing

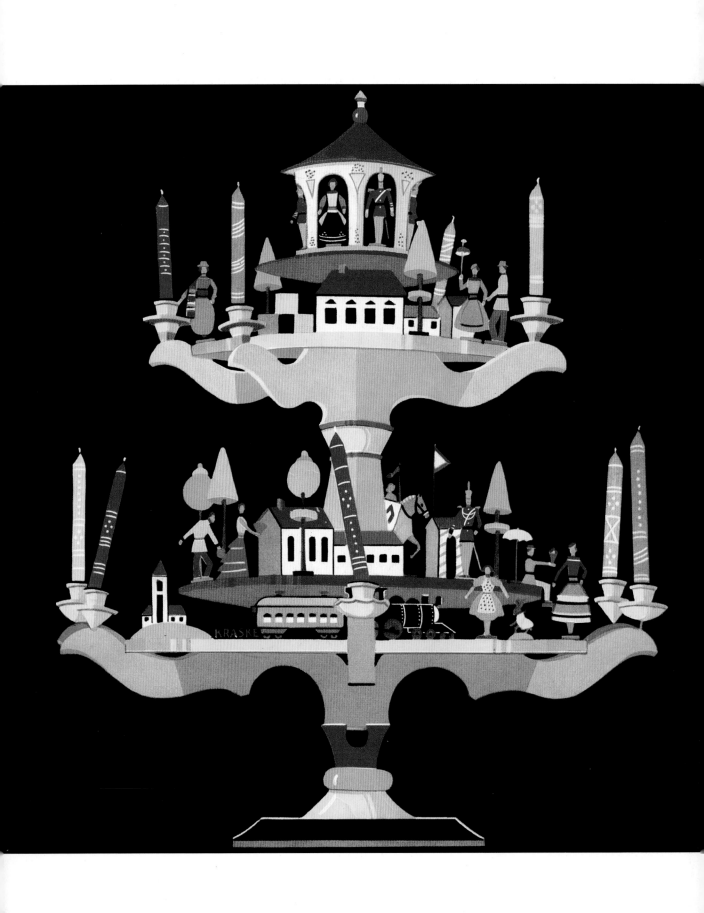

A Christmas Blessing

by Welleran Poltarnees

Blue Lantern Books
MCMXCVI

ISBN 1-883211-08-5

BLUE LANTERN BOOKS
PO BOX 4399 • SEATTLE, WASHINGTON • 98104

May this blessing fall on you
like a gentle snow.

Let your Christmas be savored
far in advance of its arrival.

May the spirit of the season
make your quest for gifts
selfless & filled with joy.

5

Adornment, reflecting old
traditions, shall make your
home bright with the loveliness
of Christmastide.

May winter, in some way,
grace your holidays.

Let there be a tree, bringing
into your home the fragrance
and power of the earth.

May song bless your Christmas,
and remind us all of the
universal harmony which is at
the center of creation.

13

In the wrapping and adornment
of your gifts, let there be the
satisfaction that all creative
acts offer.

15

On the night before Christmas
may you be visited by peace
and beneficence,

17

and visible presences who
enrich you and yours.

 19

Let the children teach you,
and all of us, through their
freshness & focus,

21

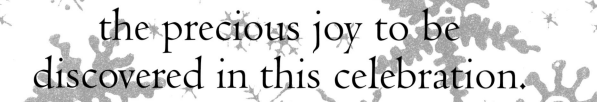

the precious joy to be
discovered in this celebration.

May you feast in
good health & comradeship.

Let us remember the
foundation of this joy—
the fear, the journey, the refuge,
the birth, the revelation.

 27

When the celebration is over
may you turn in your memory
the love, the giving and
the receiving.

from
SANTA·CLAUS.

PICTURE CREDITS

THIS BOOK WAS TYPESET IN CENTAUR.
BOOK AND COVER DESIGN BY SACHEVERELL DARLING AT BLUE LANTERN STUDIO.

PRINTED IN HONG KONG THROUGH COLORCRAFT, LTD.

Signore, dà a noi la Pace. (Is., XXVI, 12).

HEARTY
CHRISTMAS GREETINGS

MERRY CHRISTMAS

A Merrie XMAS and a Glad New YEAR.

Christmas!

A MERRY XMAS TO YOU

olly good wishes for the Christmas season